Fat-Free Writing

Business Writing for the Information Age

Carol Andrus

:50™

A Fifty-Minute™ Series Book

This Fifty-Minute™ book is designed to be "read with a pencil." It is an excellent workbook for self-study as well as classroom learning. All material is copyright-protected and cannot be duplicated without permission from the publisher. *Therefore, be sure to order a copy for every training participant by contacting:*

THOMSON
COURSE TECHNOLOGY™

■crisp CRISP series

1-800-442-7477 • 25 Thomson Place, Boston MA • www.courseilt.com

Fat-Free Writing
Business Writing for the Information Age

Carol Andrus

Credits:

Senior Editor: **Debbie Woodbury**
Copy Editor: **Charlotte Bosarge**
Assistant Editor: **Genevieve Del Rosario**
Production Manager: **Denise Powers**
Design: **Nicole Phillips**
Production Artist: **Carol Lindahl**

For more information contact:

Course Technology
25 Thomson Place
Boston, MA 02210

Or find us on the Web at **www.courseilt.com**

For permission to use material from this text or product, submit a request online at www.thomsonrights.com.

ISBN 1-56052-586-X
Library of Congress Catalog Card Number 00-104237
Printed in Canada by Webcom Limited
5 6 7 8 9 PM 06 05 04

Learning Objectives For:

FAT-FREE WRITING

The objectives for *Fat-Free Writing* are listed below. They have been developed to guide you, the reader, to the core issues covered in this book.

THE OBJECTIVES OF THIS BOOK ARE:

❑ 1) To introduce the reader to the principles of Shirtsleeve English

❑ 2) To empower the reader's writing by using verbs

❑ 3) To update the reader's style by keeping things short and simple

❑ 4) To deploy information on the page for the reader's eye

ASSESSING YOUR PROGRESS

In addition to the learning objectives above, Course Technology has developed a Crisp Series **assessment** that covers the fundamental information presented in this book. A 25-item, multiple-choice and true/false questionnaire allows the reader to evaluate his or her comprehension of the subject matter. To buy the assessment and answer key, go to www.courseilt.com and search on the book title or via the assessment format, or call 1-800-442-7477.

Assessments should not be used in any employee selection process.

Preface

Planet Earth is in the Information Age. America is no longer a smokestack economy. We're a Knowledge Economy—our biggest export is information. Today, money moves with the speed of light. Information has to move faster.

Business writing has changed radically in the last few years. Surveys show the most sought-after skill in today's business arena is: The ability to communicate clearly, correctly, and concisely, both in speech and in writing. No one has time to read long, wordy memos and letters. We all want our information faster.

While many of us are eliminating the fat from our diets and waistlines, some have yet to apply these Fat-Free principles to their communication style. Are people in your organization still writing "Pursuant to our conversation, enclosed please find the data which you requested." Or: "Should you require additional information, please do not hesitate to call our office." If they are, they're dinosaurs!

Dinosaur English costs American businesses a billion dollars a year. The language of the new millennium is *Shirtsleeve English*—simple, straightforward, to the point. That's what this short book is all about.

About the Author

Carol Andrus, president of *Write on Target*, is a speaker, writer and trainer with over 20 years of experience in language and communication training.

She holds a BA in Economics from Duke University, and an MA in Romance Languages from the University of Paris. She taught French, Spanish, and Latin in high school; served as a foreign language tour guide for New York City and was cited by the Mayor for outstanding service; has taught English to adult immigrants for the NYC Board of Education and at Baruch College.

Readers have enjoyed her articles on communication and travel in *Reader's Digest* and newspapers throughout the English-speaking world—*Chicago Tribune, Miami Herald, Seattle Times, Calcutta Statesman*—to name but a few.

In 1992, she founded *Write on Target with Carol Andrus* and has been a busy woman ever since. Clients have turned to Carol's presentations and seminars for help in communicating clearly, correctly, concisely, and confidently. She is a dynamic speaker and seminar leader, and imparts her intense love of languages and communication in an enthusiastic and inspiring manner.

Contents

Part 4: Format for Your Reader's Eye

Appendix

INTRODUCTION

2

Four Communication Styles

The psychologist Carl Jung developed a theory of human personality types, and divided them into four general categories, as shown below.

Most people are a combination of these, but one personality type is usually more dominant. In the workplace, as in daily life, we interact with people whose dominant personality type differs from our own. Take a minute to consider your written communication style. Is your style direct, informal, conversational, to the point? Or are you perhaps a bit more formal, less direct, perhaps a bit wordy?

The Doer

Description: action- and results-oriented, workaholic, competitive, decisive; firm hand-shake.

Common occupations: CEO, entrepreneur, manager, coach.

Communication style: gets right to the point; can sometimes be abrupt.

The Thinker

Description: conservative, analytical, detail-oriented; slow to make decisions.

Common occupations: accountant, lawyer, engineer.

Communication style: somewhat wordy; wants to explain the whole picture.

The Feeler

Description: people-person; friendly, warm, concerned with relationships.

Common occupations: salesperson, teacher, administrative assistant, nurse.

Communication style: persuasive, enthusiastic, creative.

The Creator

Description: scholarly, conceptual, abstract thinker.

Common occupations: scientist, researcher, artist.

Communication style: creative; takes longer to get to the point.

Three Learning Styles

We also learn in different ways—hearing, seeing, touching—and again, one style of learning is usually dominant. Can you identify your dominant learning style?

Auditory Learner Language Patterns

Verbs: hear, listen, sound, resonate, call, tell, speak

Expressions: earful; unheard of; tuned-in; manner of speaking; outspoken

Conversational clues: I hear you loud and clear. Sounds good to me. That rings a bell. How does that resonate with you? To tell the truth…

Visual Learner Language Patterns

Verbs: see, look, view, show, appear, reveal, envision, illustrate

Expressions: in my mind's eye; pretty as a picture; sight for sore eyes; take a peek

Conversational clues: I'll look into the matter. That's clear to me. I see your point. It appears to me that… Keep an eye out for….

Kinesthetic Learner Language Patterns

Verbs: feel, touch, grasp, get hold of, catch on, make contact

Expressions: come to grips with; get a handle on; get in touch with; hands-on experience; got a feel for something; pain in the neck; pull strings

Conversational clues: I feel that… Let's lay our cards on the table. I'll handle the paperwork. He's as sharp as a tack. Get a load of this.

ASSESSING YOUR COMMUNICATION STYLE

Take a few minutes to consider your own style of communication by completing this self-assessment. You may find you already have some strengths, and will discover other areas where you could use an update.

	Yes	No	Don't Know
1. Before beginning to write, I analyze my reader's needs.	❏	❏	❏
2. I tell my reader what it's about in the first sentence.	❏	❏	❏
3. I eliminate details my reader doesn't need to know.	❏	❏	❏
4. I try to keep my message to just one page.	❏	❏	❏
5. I design my page visually with lots of white space.	❏	❏	❏
6. I highlight key information for my reader's eye.	❏	❏	❏
7. I always close with an action line.	❏	❏	❏
8. I edit and proofread my document before sending it.	❏	❏	❏

Take a few minutes to evaluate yourself.

1. Some skills I already have in writing are…

_____

_____

2. Some things I find difficult in writing are…

_____

_____

3. I would be a better writer if I could…

_____

_____

A Matter of Style

Don't worry if you did not answer "yes" to every question on the previous page. As you proceed through this book, each item will be explained and illustrated with exercises that will help you make the most of your style and adjust it, where needed, for today's busy workplace.

Keep in mind that you should always write for your reader. Identify your readers' communication and learning styles and adapt to their language patterns to establish empathy and rapport. Is your reader a decision-maker, perhaps a time-pressed executive who "hears things loud and clear" and wants only bottom-line recommendations and costs before approving a project? Or perhaps a technical specialist who will "take a good look at" the complete methodology and reasoned conclusions before making a decision?

Is your relationship with business associates informal and personal, or does the situation require a more formal approach? When appropriate, adjust your style to the principles of Shirtsleeve English to fit the tone of today's fast-paced Information Age.

Consider the difference: "I would like to take this opportunity to extend my sincere congratulations on your recent appointment to the position of Vice President of the XYZ Corporation." Or: "Congratulations, John! Vice President! You've earned it. Let me treat you to lunch."

Use

Shirtsleeve

English

> *The ability to write simple direct prose that says precisely what you want it to say in the fewest words has become rare—just when business organizations have grown too large for anyone to be effective face-to-face.*
>
> **—Business Week**

Shirtsleeve Strategies

In this age of instant communication, doing more with less, and remaining nimble to stay ahead of the competition, employees must roll up their shirtsleeves and dive in at a moment's notice to adapt to changes and react to challenges. To survive in this rapid-fire environment, our tools have changed, our processes have changed, and our use of the written language has changed. To get and keep the attention of those you communicate with, you need to adopt some new writing strategies—what we call Shirtsleeve Strategies—to keep your audience engaged while they are multi-tasking and moving on to the next "opportunity" crossing their desks.

1. **Use short, familiar words.** Write to express ideas in a simple, clear manner—not to impress your reader with an extensive vocabulary or fancy writing style.

2. **Get rid of word weeds.** Our everyday speech is cluttered with habitual redundancies and unnecessary words, but they have no place in today's lean business writing.

3. **Eliminate time-wasters.** We tend to include many time-wasters simply because they are a habit. Why "on a daily basis," when "daily" will do? Or "in a timely manner," when "promptly" works. Small shortcuts save time and add clarity.

4. **Avoid stuffiness and clichés.** A good guideline for today's business writing is: If you wouldn't say it to someone in person, don't put it in writing. Use a conversational tone.

5. **Be positive in tone.** We all respond more favorably to a positive tone than to a negative tone. Negativity produces instant reader resistance.

6. **Be specific and concrete.** Vague or abstract terms do not convey immediate meaning to the reader. Use words readers can picture or that convey specific information.

7. **Don't jargonize.** Avoid unfamiliar jargon or bureaucratese, as this can confuse readers and distract from the message. Overused trendy buzzwords also weaken the message.

8. **Make items parallel.** Information is more rapidly absorbed in parallel form than when non-parallel. Parallelism also adds clarity, elegance, and symmetry to writing.

9. **Keep terms consistent.** To avoid confusing readers, use the same terms throughout the document.

Use Short, Familiar Words

Today's time-pressed readers skim for meaning, and longer or less familiar words take more time to process.

Business writing today has little use for such words as...

- ☹ peruse
- ☹ obviate
- ☹ cognizant
- ☹ remunerate

When simpler words such as...

- ☺ review
- ☺ avoid
- ☺ aware
- ☺ pay

...convey the same meaning and are faster for the eye to process.

Consider these alternatives. Which takes longer to write? Which takes longer to read?

above-mentioned	➜	this/these	in an effort to	➜	to
activate	➜	start	initially	➜	at first
additional	➜	more	modifications	➜	changes
alleviate	➜	relieve/solve	moreover	➜	besides
apprise	➜	inform	numerous	➜	several/many
approximately	➜	about	observe	➜	see
ascertain	➜	find out	on most occasions	➜	usually
benefit	➜	help	operational	➜	working
commence	➜	start/begin	optimum	➜	best
components	➜	parts	permit	➜	let
concur	➜	agree	prior to	➜	before
consequence	➜	result	provided that	➜	if
demonstrate	➜	show	request	➜	ask
determine	➜	find out	require	➜	need
encounter	➜	meet	state	➜	say
endeavor	➜	try	sufficient	➜	enough
feasible	➜	possible	terminate	➜	finish
forward	➜	send	therefore	➜	so
inasmuch as	➜	as/because	transmit	➜	send
inception	➜	start	transpire	➜	happen
initiate	➜	start/begin	witnessed	➜	saw

Note the time it takes to process these two versions of the same message. The second version uses shorter words and conveys the same meaning.

Slow: Please retain this notification with your records in the event that you are requested to furnish additional information.

Faster: Please keep this notice with your records, as we may ask for more information.

Slow: We contacted John at his residence to inquire whether we could be of assistance.

Faster: We called John at home to ask if we could help.

Slow: They encountered considerable difficulty in the retrieval of the data.

Faster: They had difficulty retrieving the data.

Remember: _____

Never utilize "utilize" when you can use "use."

GO ON A WORD DIET!

Practice reducing the fat in your writing by completing these simple exercises.

Choose simpler words:

inasmuch as _____   in regard to _____

identical _____   duplicate _____

conclude _____   subsequent to _____

equivalent _____   in the vicinity of _____

furnish _____   furthermore _____

feasible _____   kindly _____

Rewrite the following to shorten the sentences, but convey the same meaning.

1. Kindly notify me in the event that you intend to accompany us to the conference.

   _____

   _____

2. We will initiate the installation of the new software in the month of February.

   _____

   _____

3. Our computers were not operational; as a consequence, we forwarded the data to you by fax.

   _____

   _____

CONTINUED

4. We should concentrate our efforts on obtaining more advantageous terms in the contract.

_____

_____

5. The paramount concern of our department is the regulation of the new flex-time hours.

_____

_____

6. In all probability, we will elect to stay at a hotel rather than arrive early the next morning.

_____

_____

7. If we don't take immediate action to correct this problem, the ramifications could be serious.

_____

_____

8. This memo contains information of a confidential nature.

_____

_____

ANSWER KEY: GO ON A WORD DIET!

Choosing simpler words:

inasmuch as	*as/since*	in regard to	*about*
identical	*same*	duplicate	*copy*
conclude	*end/finish*	subsequent to	*after*
equivalent	*equal*	in the vicinity of	*near*
furnish	*send/give*	furthermore	*also/in*
feasible	*doable/workable*	kindly	*please*

Author's suggestions for shortening the sentences:

1. Please let me know if you plan to go to the conference with us.

2. We'll begin installing the new software in February.

3. Sorry! Our computers were down—so we faxed you the data.

4. We should focus our efforts on getting better terms in the contract.

5. Our department's main concern is regulating the new flex-time hours.

6. We will probably stay at a hotel the night before, rather than fly in early the next morning.

7. If we don't correct this problem fast, the consequences could be serious.

8. This memo contains confidential information.

Get Rid of Word Weeds

Redundancies abound in our everyday language. Common signs: "Free Gift" (gifts *are* free) and "Tattoos While U Wait." And there's always the flight attendant's announcement: "Please take your personal belongings." Leave the impersonal ones?

Today's business writing is lean, with no room for needless words. Consider these common expressions; they are full of word weeds.

true facts	**still continue**
bald-headed	**future plans**
tuna fish	**usual habit**
sum total	**unite together**
end result	**square in shape**
outer rim	**basic essentials**
honest truth	**complete monopoly**
time period	**postpone until later**
hot water heater	**serious crisis**
live audience	**advance warning**
past history	**disappear from view**
foreign imports	**brief in duration**
added bonus	**visible to the eye**
last Friday	

Other Sources of Word Weeds

Shorten wordy phrases

at a later date (later)	with regard to (about)	in order to (to)
in the event that (if)	in the near future (soon)	in the amount of (for)

More word clutter

any and all	first and foremost	each and every
if and when	whether or not	and so on and so forth

Little words can clutter too

Where is the meeting *at*?	Where are you going *to*?	He returned *back* to the office.
It fell off *of* the desk.	Help me lift this *up*.	We meet *on* Mondays.

Sometimes "-ly" is clutter

Not: firstly, secondly, most importantly

Rather: first, second, most important

Pull the Word Weeds

Practice eliminating word weeds from your writing by crossing out the unnecessary words in these sentences and revising as needed.

1. I made advance reservations at the restaurant for next Wednesday.

2. The new software is to be used only in conjunction with the MEGA program.

3. There still remain several unresolved problems to discuss.

4. Let's cooperate together so that we can reach a mutual agreement.

5. It's an actual fact that he circled around the block for an hour before finding a parking space.

6. The company bus shuttles back and forth between the corporate office and this one.

7. Research to develop new software innovations is an ongoing work in progress.

8. The problem arose at a time when we least expected it.

9. We might possibly attend the conference for a period of three days.

10. John went to the ATM machine to get some cash but he forgot his PIN number.

11. The meeting will start up at about 10AM and I'll meet you when it's over with.

12. Who's going to head up the committee?

13. Our next convention will be in the state of Nevada.

14. Where do you want this shipped to?

15. It's raining outside.

16. We cannot evaluate every single candidate.

17. I willingly agreed to oversee the project.

18. A complete list of all employees is a necessary requisite.

19. We are unable to meet the deadline at this point in time.

20. The copy machine has malfunctioned on numerous occasions.

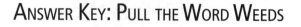

ANSWER KEY: PULL THE WORD WEEDS

1. I made ~~advance~~ reservations at the restaurant for ~~next~~ Wednesday.

2. The new software is to be used only ~~in conjunction~~ with the MEGA program.

3. There ~~still~~ remain several ~~unresolved~~ problems to discuss.

4. Let's cooperate ~~together~~ so that we can reach a*n* ~~mutual~~ agreement.

5. It's ~~an actual~~ fact that he circled ~~around~~ the block for an hour before finding a parking space.

6. The company bus shuttles ~~back and forth~~ between the corporate office and this one.

7. Research to develop ~~new~~ software innovations is ~~an ongoing~~ work in progress.

8. The problem arose ~~at a time~~ when we least expected it.

9. We might ~~possibly~~ attend the conference for ~~a period of~~ three days.

10. John went to the ATM ~~machine~~ to get some cash but he forgot his PIN ~~number~~.

11. The meeting will start ~~up~~ at ~~about~~ 10AM and I'll meet you when it's over ~~with~~.

12. Who's going to head ~~up~~ the committee?

13. Our next convention will be in ~~the state of~~ Nevada.

14. Where do you want this shipped ~~to~~?

15. It's raining ~~outside~~.

16. We cannot evaluate every ~~single~~ candidate.

17. I ~~willingly~~ agreed to oversee the project.

18. A ~~complete~~ list of all employees is a ~~necessary~~ requisite.

19. We ~~are unable to~~ *cannot* meet the deadline ~~at~~ this ~~point in time~~ week.

20. The copy machine ~~has~~ *often* malfunctione*d*~~s~~ ~~on numerous occasions~~.

Eliminate Time-Wasters

Many classic time-wasters still clog our business writing. Consider eliminating some of the following sentence-cloggers.

"the fact that…"

in view of the fact that…
in consideration of the fact that…
on account of the fact that…
owing to the fact that…
given the fact that…
} all of these could be simplified by simply using "because"

Time-waster: We canceled the picnic *due to the fact that* it was raining.

Time-saver: We canceled the picnic *because* it was raining.

Time-waster: Emma did not attend the meeting *on account of the fact that* she was ill.

Time-saver: Emma missed the meeting because she was ill.

"on a…basis."

Time-waster: We meet on a daily basis.

Time-saver: We meet every day/daily.

Time-waster: We meet on a regular basis to discuss…

Time-saver: We regularly meet to discuss…

Eliminate Time-Wasters (CONTINUED)

"in a...manner/way."

Time-waster:	...in a firm manner.
Time-saver:	...firmly.

Time-waster:	...in an efficient way.
Time-saver:	...efficiently.

"in the process of..."

Time-waster:	We are in the process of installing the new software.
Time-saver:	We are installing the new software.

Qualifiers

Words such as *very, literally, quite, somewhat, rather* contribute little—if any—meaning to business writing, and can often be eliminated.

Time-waster:	Simmons is rather well-known.
Time-saver:	Simmons is well-known.

Time-waster:	I certainly agree with you that...
Time-saver:	I agree with you that...

Time-waster:	The problems in the shipping department have been entirely eliminated.
Time-saver:	The shipping department problems have been eliminated.

Time-waster:	The scaffolding suddenly collapsed, injuring two workers rather seriously.
Time-saver:	The scaffolding collapsed, seriously injuring two workers.

"It is/was/has been…"

…and "There is/are/was/were…" add length, but no meaning.

Time-waster: There are several people waiting to be interviewed.

Time-saver: Several people are waiting to be interviewed.

Time-waster: It is our hope that the project will be brought in on deadline.

Time-saver: We hope the project will be brought in on deadline.

Reduce "of" and "that/who/which" Clutter

Time-waster: John Smith, who is the manager of our sales department, is on vacation in the month of June.

Time-saver: John Smith, our sales manager, is on vacation in June.

Time-waster: The new advertising campaign that we are developing is definitely not on schedule.

Time-saver: The new ad campaign we are developing is behind schedule.

or: Our new ad campaign is behind schedule.

Eliminate Time-Wasters (CONTINUED)

Use "Not" Sparingly

Time-waster: John was not on time.
Time-saver: John was late.

Time-waster: We do not believe…
Time-saver: We doubt…

Time-waster: Their data was not accurate.
Time-saver: Their data was inaccurate.

Small Shortcuts Save Time and Add Clarity

Eliminate unnecessary zeros, apostrophes, punctuation, and pronunciation guides on dates.

ATM's=ATMs Ph.D.=PhD $175.00=$175 1990's=1990s May 15th=May 15

Time-waster: Sue Morris will arrive next Monday, July 2nd at 10:00 A.M. in the morning, and will leave for Paris on July 5th at 8:00 P.M. in the evening.

Time-saver: Sue Morris arrives Monday, July 2 at 10am, and leaves for Paris July 5 at 8pm.

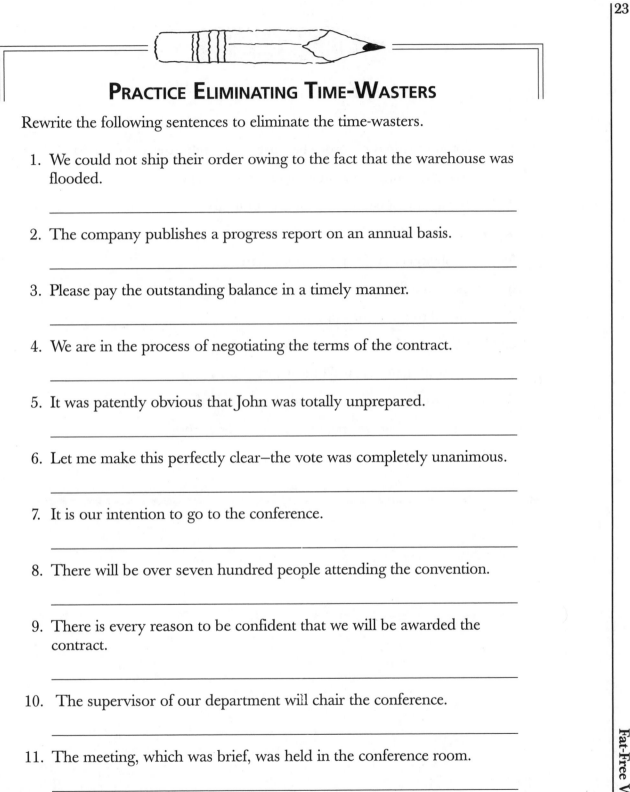

PRACTICE ELIMINATING TIME-WASTERS

Rewrite the following sentences to eliminate the time-wasters.

1. We could not ship their order owing to the fact that the warehouse was flooded.

   _____

2. The company publishes a progress report on an annual basis.

   _____

3. Please pay the outstanding balance in a timely manner.

   _____

4. We are in the process of negotiating the terms of the contract.

   _____

5. It was patently obvious that John was totally unprepared.

   _____

6. Let me make this perfectly clear—the vote was completely unanimous.

   _____

7. It is our intention to go to the conference.

   _____

8. There will be over seven hundred people attending the convention.

   _____

9. There is every reason to be confident that we will be awarded the contract.

   _____

10. The supervisor of our department will chair the conference.

    _____

11. The meeting, which was brief, was held in the conference room.

    _____

12. The terms of the contract are not acceptable.

    _____

ANSWER KEY: ELIMINATING TIME-WASTERS

1. We couldn't ship their order because the warehouse was flooded.

2. The company publishes an annual progress report.

3. Please pay the outstanding balance promptly.

4. We are negotiating the terms of the contract.

5. It was obvious that John was unprepared.

6. Let me make this clear—the vote was unanimous.

7. We intend to go to the conference.

8. Over 700 people will attend the convention.

9. We are confident that we'll be awarded the contract.

10. Our department supervisor will chair the conference.

11. The brief meeting was held in the conference room.

12. The contract terms are unacceptable.

Avoid Stuffiness and Clichés

Stuffy formality is out of date. Would you ever say to someone: "If you need additional information, please do not hesitate to call me."? Put a real person in your message. Talk directly to your reader. Use personal pronouns: I, we, you, and people's names.

Stuffy: Pursuant to our conversation, enclosed please find the agenda for the upcoming sales conference which you requested.

Real: As we discussed, enclosed is the agenda for the upcoming sales conference.

or: John, I've enclosed the sales conference agenda you asked for.

Stuffy: We wish to take this opportunity to thank you for your participation in our recent fund-raising campaign for the animal shelter.

Real: Thank you, Mrs. Sanchez, for helping us raise over $35,000 for the animal shelter!

TALK TO YOUR READER

Rewrite these in a more conversational tone.

1. This is to acknowledge receipt of your letter of May 12th in which you requested our new product brochure.

   _____

   _____

2. Attached hereto please find my check in the amount of $125.00.

   _____

   _____

3. Kindly remit the outstanding balance by June 15th.

   _____

   _____

4. Should you require additional information, please do not hesitate to call me.

   _____

   _____

CONTINUED

Rewrite this stuffy form letter.

> Enclosed please find your endorsement effective April 1st, 2000 amending your home insurance policy. Please review the enclosure carefully, duly noting all terms, conditions, and exclusions. The endorsement should then be attached to your policy. If you should discover any discrepancies, please advise our office immediately. Should you have any questions, please do not hesitate to call our office.
>
> It is always our pleasure to service all of your insurance needs.

Your conversational letter:

Author's suggested responses can be found in the Appendix.

Be Positive in Tone

We all respond more favorably to a positive tone than to a negative tone. Negativity produces instant reader resistance. Consider these:

Negative: No smoking anywhere except the bar!
Positive: Smoking permitted in the bar only.

Negative: Positively no children admitted without an adult!
Positive: Children welcome when accompanied by an adult.

Negative: We cannot process applications received after June 10.
Positive: Please return the application before the June 10 deadline.

Avoid Negative Buzzwords

Some negative words convey an immediate strong resistance in the reader. Consider your reaction to these powerful words:

botched	misleading
deceptive	regrettable
false	rude
incident	second-rate
incompetent	shoddy
inconsiderate	thoughtless
inept	uncooperative
infuriating	unfounded
mishandled	unprofessional
misinformed	unqualified

Use Positive Words

Positive words can convey the same message, and will elicit a more cooperative reaction from your reader. Notice the difference in tone.

"You *claim* that…"	vs.	"You tell us that…" *or* "You state that…"
"You *fail* to see…"	vs.	"May I point out that…"
"You *neglected* to send…"	vs.	"Your check was not enclosed."
"the *alleged* incident"	vs.	"the incident you refer to"

Negative Apologies Leave a Negative Impression

Affirm your reader's right to complain and state positively what you will do to rectify a mistake.

Negative: We're sorry this mistake occurred.

Positive: You are right in pointing out that…

Negative: We are indeed sorry the information was sent to the wrong person.

Positive: We'll make sure the information gets to you next time.

WHICH PICNIC WOULD YOU RATHER ATTEND?

This one...

> TO: All Employees
>
> FROM: Human Resources
>
> RE: The Company Picnic
>
> This year our annual company picnic will take place on Friday, July 2nd. According to our new company policy, this year employees will be permitted to invite members of their immediate families to attend. As we have signed up for a park picnic area, it is imperative that we know the number of people who plan to attend. If you plan to do so, please sign the attached list and put the number of family members you plan to invite. Employees who have not signed up will not be permitted to attend.
>
> Thank you for your cooperation.

Or this one?

> TO: All Employees
>
> FROM: Dinah Myte - Human Resources
>
> RE: OUR COMPANY PICNIC - FRIDAY, JULY 2!
>
> We are all looking forward to our annual company picnic. This year, due to overwhelming demand, employees may invite family members.
>
> We have reserved a lovely picnic area near the Marina in Riverside Park. So that we will be able to provide seating and food for all, we will need to know the number of people attending.
>
> If you plan to attend:
>
> • Print your full name on this list.
>
> • Note the total number of people in your party.
>
> • Return this list to the receptionist.
>
> SEE YOU AT THE PICNIC!

PRACTICE BEING POSITIVE

Rewrite these sentences using a more positive tone.

1. We do not deliver after 11pm.

_____

2. Please do not violate the safety codes.

_____

3. If payment is not received by May 1, there will be an added penalty.

_____

4. Your order cannot be shipped until your payment has been received.

_____

5. Please do not forget to send this quarter's sales figures before the 15th.

_____

6. Your credit limit may not exceed $5,000.

_____

Rewrite this letter in a more positive tone.

> Attached hereto is a Policyholder's Report form which was previously sent to you, but you neglected to complete and return it to us. It is imperative that you complete and return this form promptly. The company will make no adjustment to your premium until the completed form has been returned.
>
> Please do not hesitate to contact our office should you require assistance in completing this form.

Your positive rewrite:

Author's suggested responses can be found in the Appendix.

Be Specific and Concrete

Vague or abstract terms do not convey an immediate meaning to your reader. Use words readers can picture or that convey specific information.

Which answer gives the reader an immediate mental picture?

Question: "How big is an acre?"

Answer #1: An acre is 4,840 square yards, or 43,560 square feet.

Answer #2: It's a football field minus the end zones!

Notice the difference in the two versions:

Vague: The new advertising campaign will have a substantial effect on sales.

Specific: The new ad campaign will increase sales by at least 15%.

Vague: A majority of our employees voted in favor of flex-time scheduling.

Specific: Over 90% of our employees voted for flex-time scheduling.

Vague: The employee training program has a very good attendance record.

Specific: The employee training program has a 95% attendance record.

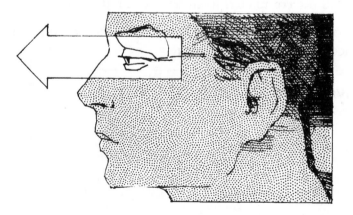

Always set a deadline, even if you have to "invent" one!

Vague: Please print 20 copies of this report for me as soon as possible.

Specific: Dan, I'll be very grateful if I can have 20 copies of this report by Monday.

Vague: Please return this at your earliest convenience.

Specific: _____

_____

Vague: May we meet to discuss this sometime in the near future?

Specific: _____

_____

Please return this to me by Monday.

May we meet to discuss this early next week? I'll call to set up an appointment.

Don't Jargonize

Avoid unfamiliar jargon or bureaucratese, as this can confuse readers and distract attention from your real message. Overused, trendy words also weaken your message. The US government is famous for inscrutable jargon, such as this sign in a Federal government building: *"All illumination on these premises must be extinguished upon departure."* Why not simply: *"Please turn out the lights if you're the last to leave!"*

Gobbledygook

Sign in an office building: Food Not To Be Taken Internally!

Board-of-Educationese: This fall there will be a negative increase in school enrollment.

Performance Appraisal: This employee is recommended for negative advancement.

Wall Street memo: Some 400 employees will be subject to our negative employee retention policy.

US Census Bureau term for "homeless people":   targeted nonsheltered outdoor-location people

Could Anyone Figure These Out?

"Our proactive client-focused strategies have led to synchronized benchmark enhancement of our value-added bottom-line facilitation for customer satisfaction."

"Our global win-win strategy, in conjunction with our new on-demand outside-the-box game plan, will ramp up vertical-market empowerment."

Speaking of Jargonize…

Practice restraint in using "-ize" as a shortcut.

It used to be we "offered an apology" to someone we offended and "gave the eulogy" at a funeral. Today we apologize, eulogize, customize, optimize, prioritize. However, there are limits. The following are examples of awkward and distracting uses of "ize."

Newspaper obituary:	He will be funeralized Friday.
Insurance bulletin:	This new legislation will disasterize the insurance industry.
Letter from a lawyer:	This is to awarize you that…
Coptalk:	Three buildings were arsonized.
Newspaper:	Some countries are dollarizing their currencies.

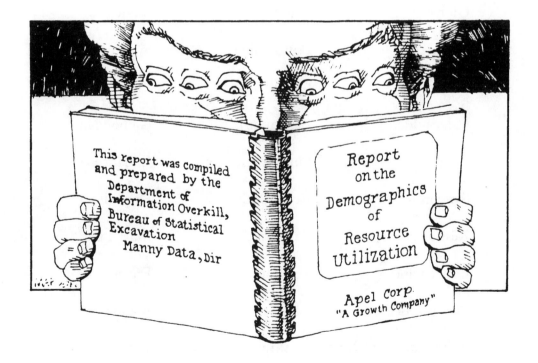

TIME TO DE-JARGONIZE

Learn to recognize inscrutable jargon by practicing writing it. Then banish this bad habit from your own writing.

First Be Aware

Writing a progress report with no progress to report? Here's how to impress and bamboozle your readers simultaneously. Choose a term from each column below and create a sentence of inscrutable jargon. Be creative!

_____

_____

Column 1	Column 2	Column 3
Virtual	Support	Partnering
Global	Win-win	Strategies
Balanced	Bottom-line	Synergy
Fast-track	Quality-driven	Empowerment
Value-added	Benchmark	Game Plan
Proactive	Outside-the-box	Enhancement
Synchronized	Reciprocal	Firewall
Result-driven	Bandwidth	Marketing
On-demand	Vertical-market	Facilitation
Best Practice	Client-focused	Alliances

CONTINUED

Then Beware

De-jargonize these sentences so that the meaning is immediately clear to the reader.

1. The supervisor will interface with the union representatives on Thursday.

   _____

   _____

2. We will attempt to facilitate as is feasible.

   _____

   _____

3. The company bus provides connectivity between our Miami and Ft. Lauderdale offices.

   _____

   _____

4. Employees who come in late will be subject to our disincentive policy.

   _____

   _____

5. In order to obtain optimum fuel mileage, maintain speed at 55mph or below.

   _____

   _____

6. She answered in the negative.

   _____

   _____

Author's suggested responses can be found in the Appendix.

Make Items Parallel

Information is more rapidly absorbed in parallel form than when non-parallel. Items in a series should be in the same form: nouns followed by nouns; adjectives by adjectives. Parallelism also adds clarity, elegance, and symmetry to writing.

Awkward: "Hey, buddies …all you guys out there in Rome…my compatriots…listen to me!"

Elegant: "Friends, Romans, Countrymen, lend me your ears!"

Examples of effective parallel construction:

"I stand before you today, the representative of a family in grief, in a country in mourning, before a world in shock." –Earl Spencer, *Princess Diana's Eulogy*

"Puritanism is the haunting fear that someone, somewhere, sometime, may be happy." –H. L. Mencken

"My team is agile, mobile and…hostile!" –football coach

CHILDREN ON BOARD–PARENTS ON VALIUM! –bumper sticker

BIG ENOUGH TO DO THE JOB!–SMALL ENOUGH TO CARE!
–sign on a moving van

Note the Differences

Non-parallel: "Ask what you can do for your country—not the other way around!"

Parallel: "Ask not what your country can do for you. Ask what you can do for your country."   —President John Kennedy

Non-parallel: "I come to bury Caesar. I didn't come to give him praise."
Parallel: "I come to bury Caesar, not to praise him!"
—Shakespeare, *Julius Caesar*

Non-parallel: The graphics department has started using the new software and to produce great designs.

Parallel: The graphics department has started *using* the new software and *producing* great designs.

Non-parallel: We will have to decide which files to put in storage and the ones to delete.

Parallel: We will have to decide *which files* to put in storage and *which ones* to delete.

Make Items in Lists Parallel

Lists are faster to process when items are parallel.

Not:	**Rather:**
These items will be discussed at the meeting:	These items will be discussed at the meeting:
1. *When* to announce the new acquisition	1. *When* to announce the new acquisition
2. *Where* to hold our next convention	2. *Where* to hold our next convention
3. *Methods* to improve employee morale	3. *How* to improve employee morale

Make Items in Procedures and Directions Parallel

Parallel procedures and directions are easier to follow. Use verbs. Tell people what to do.

Not:

Procedure for entering the building after 6pm:

1. The entrance on Fulton Street should be used.
2. At the right of the door, enter your employee ID# on the security pad.
3. The security guard will come to the door.
4. Show the guard your ID badge.
5. Once admitted to the building, the sign-in sheet must be filled in.

But:

Follow this procedure to enter the building after 6pm:

1. Go to the entrance on Fulton Street.

2. Enter your employee ID# on the security pad at the right of the door.

3. Wait for the security guard.

4. Show the guard your ID badge.

5. Once admitted to the building, fill in the sign-in sheet.

CONSTRUCTING PARALLEL SENTENCES

Rewrite these sentences in parallel form.

1. Forms should be read first, accurately completed, and then you should return them to us.

   _____

   _____

2. Joan was concerned about salary, security, and to be able to advance on the job.

   _____

   _____

3. Bob enjoys skiing, hiking, and to camp in the mountains on the weekends.

   _____

   _____

4. I found it easier to write the report than editing it.

   _____

   _____

5. This year's sales were better than last year.

   _____

   _____

6. John handled the crisis quickly, thoroughly and he was very professional.

   _____

   _____

7. His lack of enthusiasm is disappointing, frustrating, and it annoys everyone.

   _____

   _____

Author's suggested responses can be found in the Appendix.

Keep Terms Consistent

To avoid confusing readers, use the same terms throughout the document. The following passage is a real-life example of total confusion.

> To the Stockholders of XYZ, Inc.:
>
> Enclosed you will find stock certificates representing the additional shares of Common Stock of XYZ, Inc. to which you are entitled pursuant to the twenty-five (25%) percent stock dividend which was declared to holders of record of XYZ's Common Stock at the close of business on November 27, 1991. The number of shares reflected on the new dividend certificates has been determined by multiplying the number of shares which you held as of the record date by one-fourth. Your previous stock dividend certificates will continue to represent the same number of shares of Common Stock as heretofore. There is no need for you to exchange them for new record certificates. If you had been a holder of Preferred Stock, you would have been entitled to a dividend check.

Notice that "stock certificate" becomes "dividend certificate," then "stock dividend certificate," and finally, "record certificate"—a total of four different terms for a single piece of paper. The company was besieged by hundreds of calls from confused recipients.

IDENTIFY AND CORRECT INCONSISTENCIES

Correct the inconsistent term.

We have decided to begin publishing a monthly inter-divisional newsletter. Your comments, suggestions and contributions are welcome, and should be emailed to Maude Dennis before the 15th of the month. The first issue of the news bulletin will be on July 1. We look forward to receiving your contributions.

ANSWER KEY: IDENTIFY AND CORRECT INCONSISTENCIES

The use of the terms "newsletter" and "news bulletin" are inconsistent.
Pick one and use it in both places.

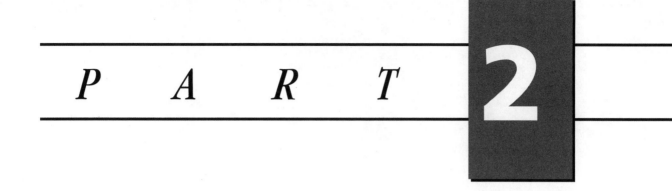

Use Power

Language

> *"Clear powerful writing is a survival skill in today's marketplace."*
>
> —**Wall Street Journal**

Verbs Are Power Words

Napoleon, one of history's human dynamos, often referred to himself as "un verbe!" Verbs express action (run, jump, yell, point) or a state of being (is, seems, feels) and tell us what is happening. Verbs are, however, frequently disempowered by being put into passive voice or noun form. Use these techniques to empower your words and your writing.

➤ **Use active voice.** There are over 6,000 languages spoken on planet Earth, and they all have passive voice–because it serves a purpose. It does, however, take longer for the reader to process.

➤ **Go for the verb.** Verbs can lose power by being turned into nouns, and this is also harder for the reader to process.

➤ **Avoid wimp-speak.** Be specific about what you want, what you will do, what you expect.

Remember: _____

Immediate clarity is the benchmark of good business writing.

Use Active Voice

In passive voice, the subject receives the action of the verb. There are three general categories where the passive voice is used:

1. When the "doer" is unknown:

   "The files were accidentally deleted."   "My car was stolen."

2. When the "doer" is unimportant:

   "The game was canceled due to the snowstorm."

3. When you need to be diplomatic (i.e., not "blame" someone):

   Think again: "The boss made a big mistake!"

   Diplomatic: "Perhaps an error has been made."

Passive voice is impersonal and eliminates the "doer." It can be used in a message of refusal to distance the doer from "blame."

Active:	The Board *must* deny your request for transfer.
Passive:	Your request for transfer *must be denied.*
Active:	We *must postpone* settlement of your claim as you have not yet filed the accident report.
Passive:	The settlement of your claim *must be postponed* until the accident report has been filed.

Which is faster to process?

Passive:	The ball was kicked by John.
Active:	John kicked the ball.
Passive:	When market tests *were performed,* it *was discovered* that strong sales *will be generated* by the new product line.
Active:	Market tests *show* that the new product line *will SELL!*
Passive:	The ballots *will be collected* by the secretary and *counted* by the treasurer.
Active:	The secretary *will collect* the ballots and the treasurer *will count* them.

PRACTICE THE ACTIVE APPROACH

Edit these sentences to change the passive verbs to active voice.

1. Your order will be shipped as soon as your payment is received.
2. The meeting will be attended by all employees.
3. The conveyor belt was repaired by the engineer.
4. The delivery dates have been confirmed by the shipping department.
5. The research was compiled by Bruce Graham, and the report was written by Mark Ayton.

Rewrite the following memo in active voice.

TO: All New Employees

FROM: Human Resources

RE: Employee Health Records

All health records of new employees should be sent to the central records office by January 5. Records of immunization and vaccinations should be included. Records should be sent to the attention of Kate Smith.

If these records are not received by the above date, health coverage cannot be guaranteed.

If more information is needed, please call John Jones, Ext. 123.

Your active version:

Author's suggested responses can be found in the Appendix.

Go for the Verb!

Verbs are frequently disempowered by being turned into nouns (nounized?) by adding -tion; -ence; -ment.

Keep It Simple

Take advantage of the power of verbs and resist turning them into nouns. Not only will your sentences be more powerful, they will also be shorter. Consider these:

reach an agreement	➔	agree
bring to a conclusion	➔	conclude/finish/end
gave an explanation	➔	explained
give assistance	➔	assist/help/aid
placed an order	➔	ordered
offer a suggestion	➔	suggest
have need for	➔	need
commit an error	➔	err
file an application	➔	apply
take action	➔	act
conduct an investigation	➔	investigate
hold a meeting	➔	meet

Keep in mind that Shirtsleeve English has the advantage of grabbing and holding the reader's attention because is it quicker to read and easier to process. Which of the two versions below take longer to process?

❑ We *had a discussion* with Jake Mason about the problems in the inventory department.

❑ We discussed the inventory department problems with Jake Mason.

❑ Dr. Larson *has a tendency* to make speeches that are long in length.

❑ Dr. Larson tends to make long speeches.

Keep It Direct

The verb *make* often disguises the real action. Why "make a decision" when you can go directly for the verb and simply *decide*.

make a recommendation ➜ recommend

make use of ➜ use

make mention of ➜ mention

make revisions ➜ revise

make an adjustment ➜ adjust

make contact with ➜ contact

Which of the two versions below take longer to process?

❑ *We made inquiry* regarding discounts for registered dealers.

❑ We inquired about discounts for registered dealers.
   or We asked about discounts for registered dealers.

❑ The new health-care policy *will make provision for* employees who work part time.

❑ The new health-care policy will provide for part-time employees.

Avoid Wimp-Speak

As George Eliot said in *Middlemarch:* "Might, could, would—they are contemptible auxiliaries." Readers respond to clear, direct language. Tell them in specific language what you will do or what you want them to do.

Wimp-Speak	Power-Speak
"I feel that…"	"I think that…"
"I believe that…"	"I am confident that…"
"I'll try to…"	"I will…" or "I'll…"
"…should be done"	"Please do…"
"Action should be taken to…"	"Let's take action to…"
"…must be submitted"	"Please submit by…"
"Forms should go to HR."	"Please send the forms to HR."
"This should be discussed…"	"Let's discuss this Thursday over lunch."

EMPOWER YOUR VERBS

In each of these examples, the real action verbs have been disguised as nouns. Circle the weak nouns in each sentence and then rewrite the sentence using a power verb.

1. The Board of Directors made a decision to cancel the project.

   _____

2. We gave careful consideration to this proposal.

   _____

3. He made reference to recent data from the XYZ Corp.

   _____

CONTINUED

4. The sysop made a recommendation that we purchase the software.

_____

5. The chemist performed an analysis of the new specimens.

_____

6. Jones was not successful in making contact with the XYZ sales reps.

_____

7. The accountant performed an audit on the accounts.

_____

8. He gave no indication which format he had a preference for.

_____

9. Not meeting the deadline will put the program in jeopardy.

_____

10. The technical vocabulary of the report causes readers confusion.

_____

11. The contractor was not in compliance with the building code.

_____

12. I'll make every effort to finish the research by Friday.

_____

13. We are planning on going to the marketing conference in May.

_____

14. The CEO made a speech at the convention.

_____

15. I hope this meets with your approval.

_____

ANSWER KEY: EMPOWER YOUR VERBS

1. The Board of Directors decided…

2. We carefully considered…

3. He referred…

4. The sysop recommended…

5. The chemist analyzed…

6. Jones couldn't contact…

7. The accountant audited…

8. He didn't indicate which format he preferred.

9. Not meeting the deadline will jeopardize the program.

10. The technical vocabulary of the report confuses readers.

11. The contractor did not comply…

12. I'll finish the research by Friday.

13. We are going to the marketing conference in May.

14. The CEO spoke at the convention.

15. I hope you approve.

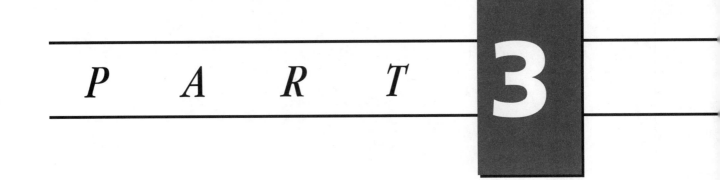

K.I.S.S.—

Keep It Short

& Simple!

" *Difficult concepts, particularly, benefit from simple language. The ability to express them simply is a sign of brilliance.*"

–John Beckley, **The Power of Little Words**

It Is Simply Faster

Effective business writing today is 10th grade level, not because businesspeople are less educated, but because we all want our information faster. Malcolm Forbes (whose "doer" communication style was always direct and to the point) once commented: "I read 10,000 business documents a year. You can't make it too simple for me!"

Today, readers scan for meaning. Extensive research has been done on how the human eye processes written information—and K.I.S.S. is the key. Keep it short and simple: shorter words, shorter sentences, shorter paragraphs. Email has ushered in an unprecedented new informality in written language, and this has extended to paper writing—memos, letters, reports.

Write Shorter Sentences

Lengthy, complicated sentences with lots of punctuation take longer to process.

Average sentence length in business writing today

Easy:	8-11 words
Standard:	12-16 words
Difficult:	21+ words

What does the following 81-word sentence really say?

> "It is the policy of this company that all account service personnel are required to review and adhere to the pricing structure which is in place for projects that include technology participation and as always verification should be made as to the current standing contract to ensure that the distributor does not have special rates in place, which, if said contract stipulates DS support at a specific rate, that rate is required to be honored for the term of the contract."

❑ It is company policy not to honor contract agreements.

❑ Please note: For projects that include technology participation, account reps should review distributor contracts to see if special rates are stipulated. If so, we must honor these rates for the term of the contract.

❑ All employees must wash their hands before leaving the lab.

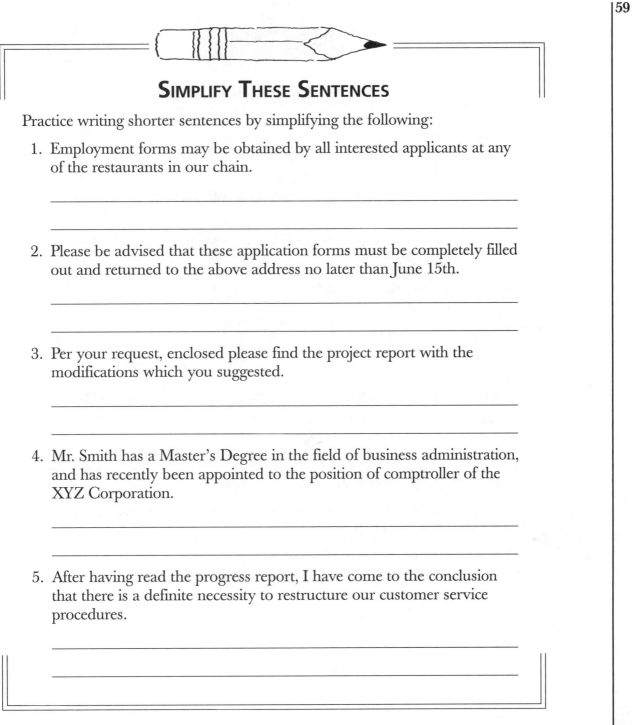

SIMPLIFY THESE SENTENCES

Practice writing shorter sentences by simplifying the following:

1. Employment forms may be obtained by all interested applicants at any of the restaurants in our chain.

   _____

   _____

2. Please be advised that these application forms must be completely filled out and returned to the above address no later than June 15th.

   _____

   _____

3. Per your request, enclosed please find the project report with the modifications which you suggested.

   _____

   _____

4. Mr. Smith has a Master's Degree in the field of business administration, and has recently been appointed to the position of comptroller of the XYZ Corporation.

   _____

   _____

5. After having read the progress report, I have come to the conclusion that there is a definite necessity to restructure our customer service procedures.

   _____

   _____

Answer Key: Simplifying Sentences

1. If you are interested in applying, go to any of our restaurants for employment forms.

   or: Employment forms are available at all our restaurants.

2. Please return the completed application forms before June 15.

3. As you requested, enclosed is the project report with the changes you suggested.

   or: Here's the new version of the project report. Thanks for the great suggestions!

4. Mr. Smith has an MBA (or a Master's in Business Administration) and has recently been appointed controller of the XYZ Corporation.

5. After reading the progress report, I see we need to restructure our customer service procedures.

   or: Having read the progress report, I see we need to restructure our customer service procedures.

Create Must-Read Reference Lines

Put specific information in the Regarding (RE:) or Subject line to tell your reader what to expect. Think of it as a "Purpose Line."

Typical: RE: Employee Health Coverage

Better: RE: Important Changes in Employee Health Coverage

Typical: RE: Vacation Date Requests

Better: RE: Feb 5—Deadline for Vacation Date Requests!

Write a Purpose Line for each of the following:

Re: _____

Because of numerous customer complaints about late deliveries, I recently visited the warehouse. I found it in poor condition. The loading equipment and delivery trucks are not serviced regularly, causing frequent breakdowns. The conveyor belt to the loading dock needs replacing. We need to meet with the acting manager (the regular manager is on extended sick leave) to review maintenance schedules and arrange for a new conveyor belt.

Subject: _____

It is with great pleasure that we extend an invitation to all our distributors to attend our New Product Line Presentation Luncheon—Wednesday, March 14, 11:30am-3pm, in the Grand Ballroom of the Sheraton Plaza Hotel, Seventh Avenue at 50th Street, NYC. Please RSVP to Sally Milford at 555-1212.

Author's suggested responses can be found in the Appendix.

Email subject lines

Providing complete yet concise purpose lines is especially important for email. The email subject line can determine if and when the recipient opens and reads the message. Don't overuse "Urgent" and keep the subject line short—most are only 25 spaces.

Re: _____

Joe, please note that the budget meeting scheduled for tomorrow at 2pm has been changed to 10am and will now meet in the Board Room on the 5th floor (Room 510). I left you a message on voicemail, but could not be sure you would get it in time. Please confirm receipt of this as your attendance at this meeting is of prime importance. We need you there to support our position!

Author's suggested responses can be found in the Appendix.

Get Right to the Point

The opening statement in your document must be powerful enough to grab and hold the reader's attention. Tell the reader the important *who, what, when, why, where,* or *how* in the first sentence. Here are a few techniques for getting right to the point.

Identify Yourself—Make the Connection

It was a great pleasure speaking with you at the NSA convention.

Jack Garson, our garage manager, has asked me to reply to your letter concerning the damage to your car while it was parked in our garage.

State Your Purpose Up Front

Everyone please note: installation of the new equipment in the cafeteria will be delayed, so we have developed these alternative plans for minimum disruption.

We have corrected the error in your billing, Mr. Carlson. The new balance shows…

Can we meet Monday morning to discuss the following problems with the Morton account:

Ask an Attention-Grabbing Question

When are we going to get some healthful food in our cafeteria?

Ms. Jones…are you aware that your car insurance has expired?

Get Right to the Point (CONTINUED)

Ask for Action Up Front

Please review these sales figures, Sarah, and let me have your feedback by Friday.

We are in urgent need of repairs to our apartment.

Establish Goodwill

Thank you for taking the time to write us about this problem, Mr. Jimenez.

You're right, Mrs. Anderson—we did send you the wrong color sheet set!

Make a Challenging Offer

Enclosed is a FREE 30-day sample of our new VitaPep Product—no strings attached!

We can cut your cable TV costs by 50%!

Close with a Bang!

As with the opening statement, your closing statement should also be powerful and reinforce the purpose of the document. Some readers will skim a message by reading only the beginning and then skipping to the end. Make sure the closing serves your purpose.

Tell the Reader What to Do

I'll be very grateful if you can get this data to me before Friday, Joe. Thanks!

If you need to discuss this, just give me a call. My direct line is 212-555-1212.

So, Mrs. Hanover, if our offer sounds interesting, just drop the enclosed postcard in the mail.

Tell the Reader What You Will Do

Again, Ms. Dye, pardon our delay. We'll have your new computer to you by July 15.

I'll call you early Monday morning so that we can finalize this.

As soon as you confirm the dates, we'll book our flight reservations.

Close with Goodwill

Thanks again for bringing this important matter to our attention, Mrs. Jones.

Our very best wishes for great success with your new business!

Write Shorter Paragraphs

In Shirtsleeve English, paragraphs should be a maximum of six or seven lines, or two to four sentences. Anything longer is hard to process. Respect your reader's time. Edit ruthlessly to eliminate details your reader doesn't need to know. Avoid a rambling conversation on the screen or page.

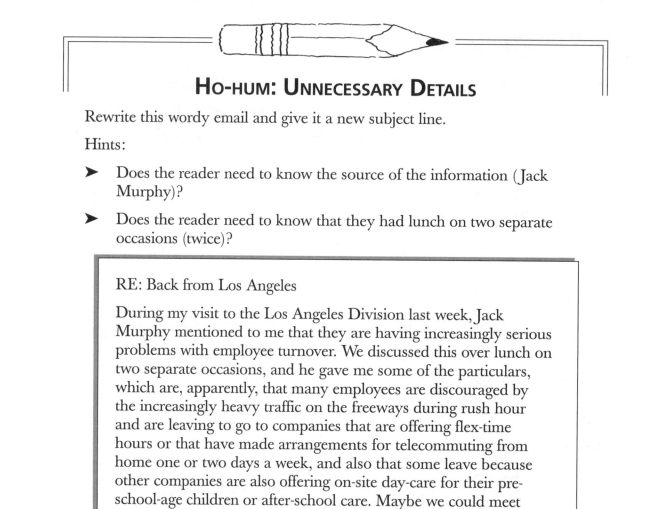

HO-HUM: UNNECESSARY DETAILS

Rewrite this wordy email and give it a new subject line.

Hints:

➤ Does the reader need to know the source of the information (Jack Murphy)?

➤ Does the reader need to know that they had lunch on two separate occasions (twice)?

RE: Back from Los Angeles

During my visit to the Los Angeles Division last week, Jack Murphy mentioned to me that they are having increasingly serious problems with employee turnover. We discussed this over lunch on two separate occasions, and he gave me some of the particulars, which are, apparently, that many employees are discouraged by the increasingly heavy traffic on the freeways during rush hour and are leaving to go to companies that are offering flex-time hours or that have made arrangements for telecommuting from home one or two days a week, and also that some leave because other companies are also offering on-site day-care for their pre-school-age children or after-school care. Maybe we could meet sometime next week to discuss the possibility of implementing some or all of these programs to reduce this serious loss of highly skilled employees. (144 words)

CONTINUED

—————————————CONTINUED—————————————

Your rewrite:

Author's suggested responses can be found in the Appendix.

Use Transitions

As your reader skims through text, transitions act as instant road signs to tell them where you are heading. *Also* tells the reader that you are adding a similar thought. *However* instantly conveys "here comes something different."

Purpose	**Transitions**
To add an idea	*Also, and, besides, furthermore, moreover, next, too, as well as, in addition, again*
To summarize	*In brief, on the whole, in short, in sum, to sum up*
To enumerate	*First, second, third, and last*
To clarify	*Actually, in other words, clearly*
To illustrate	*For instance, for example (e.g.,), that is (i.e.,)*
To compare	*Also, similarly, likewise, as well as*
To contrast	*Although, even though, but, however, on the contrary, on the other hand, yet, in contrast*
To emphasize	*Certainly, most of all, in fact, of course, in any event*
To make conditional	*If, unless, until, when, even though*
To show cause and effect	*As a result, so, therefore, consequently, accordingly*
To show results	*As a result, therefore, so, hence*
To reverse a thought	*But, yet, on the contrary, regardless, nevertheless*
To indicate time or sequence	*Formerly, previously, meanwhile, before, after, until now, at the same time, later, during*

Sentences and phrases can also serve as transitions

"That brings us to the next step, which is…"

"Now that we've settled that problem, let's look at…"

"Unfortunately, in this case, we won't be able to…"

"In addition to budget constraints, there's another matter we have to discuss."

In the following example, note the opening, which identifies the purpose, and the use of transitions.

Dear Mr. Harper:

As you requested during our recent phone conversation, I've itemized below an explanation which should clarify the increase in our billing for the landscaping, and the lawn and tree maintenance work we have done for you this year.

Briefly, our hourly rate has increased since last year from $50 to $65. Also, this year you requested weekly lawn maintenance, as compared to last year, when maintenance was every two weeks.

In addition, you may recall that earlier this year you requested that we send our tree crew to prune and spray your fruit trees every six months, whereas last year the trees were pruned and sprayed only once.

Finally, two of your apple trees were infected with bark rust and, at your request, were treated by our tree surgeon, which required six visits.

In closing, Mr. Harper, we hope this explanation is satisfactory. If you have questions or wish to discuss or renegotiate the level of services that you are receiving from our firm, we would be happy to arrange an appointment. Please call me at 555-1234.

We appreciate your business and look forward to continued service.

Very sincerely,

PRACTICE USING TRANSITIONS

In the following message, supply transitions that will serve as road signs and help guide the reader through the memo.

Dear Marvin: It is with great sadness that I must decline your gracious invitation to the Grand Opening of your new restaurant in New York City on March 12. There are several reasons why I will not be able to celebrate this wonderful occasion with you.

_____, I will be in Singapore attending the Asian Chamber of Commerce International Convention from March 7-9, and will be returning to California on the 10th.

_____, jet-lag notwithstanding, at 8AM the morning of the 11th, I am scheduled to present the new Budget Proposal Package to our Board of Directors, and _____, and perhaps _____ _____, the weekend of March 12-13, is our annual family reunion in Pasadena, and over 200 family members are coming from all points on planet Earth.

_____, just to mark the occasion, something very special—a fond remembrance from our college days—will be delivered on opening day!

I know your new restaurant will be, as usual, a great success. Stay in touch!

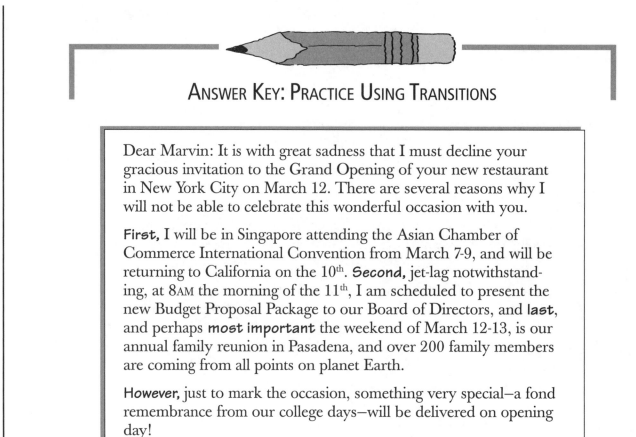

ANSWER KEY: PRACTICE USING TRANSITIONS

Dear Marvin: It is with great sadness that I must decline your gracious invitation to the Grand Opening of your new restaurant in New York City on March 12. There are several reasons why I will not be able to celebrate this wonderful occasion with you.

First, I will be in Singapore attending the Asian Chamber of Commerce International Convention from March 7-9, and will be returning to California on the 10th. **Second,** jet-lag notwithstanding, at 8AM the morning of the 11th, I am scheduled to present the new Budget Proposal Package to our Board of Directors, and **last,** and perhaps **most important** the weekend of March 12-13, is our annual family reunion in Pasadena, and over 200 family members are coming from all points on planet Earth.

However, just to mark the occasion, something very special—a fond remembrance from our college days—will be delivered on opening day!

I know your new restaurant will be, as usual, a great success. Stay in touch!

Format for

Your

Reader's Eye

Don't send me thick gray clouds on the page! My time is valuable. Direct my eyes to the important stuff."

—Jack Beason, NYC Insurance Broker

Design Your Page Visually

Use lists, headings, labels, bullets, bolding, underlining, design aids, graphic lines—all the wonderful inserts available in our computers—to guide your reader's eye to important information. Just be careful not to overdo this and clutter or distract from your message.

You may want to consider using eye-catching symbols available on your computer, such as these:

✔   ☞   ✖   ➔   ☺   ☹   ∂   ≠   ✐

Keep in mind that spacing is also a visual tool for highlighting information. Leave lots of white space. Make your message leap off the page!

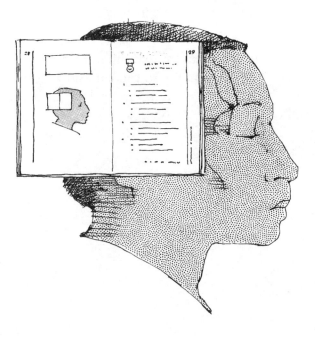

Use Headings and Labels

Highlight the main point of your message by creating a simple header. Break up paragraphs of text by using subheads. Clarify sections of information or graphics by including labels and captions. Here are some suggestions.

Problem(s)	Purpose	Background	Recommendation(s)
Solution	Advantages	Disadvantages	Implications
Action to Take	Costs	Next Step	Example
Alternative(s)	Benefits	Findings	Decisions
Observations	Options	Summary	Supporting Data
Directions	Instructions	Conclusions	If/Then
Scope of study	Results	Considerations	Sequence of Events

In the example on the facing page, headings are used to capture the reader's attention and encourage this person to consider solutions to the writer's complaint.

Notice that the two paragraphs are justified differently: The "problem" paragraph is fully "justified" (aligns equally to the left and right margins). As such, it is harder to read. The "solutions" paragraph is left-justified only. Research shows that left-justified is easier to read.

Dear Executive Director,

I am a disabled person and come to your hospital three times a week for physical therapy and I need your help in solving a recurring dilemma.

Here's My Problem

Even though there are several parking spaces near the entrance reserved for people with disabilities, there are never any spaces available to park. Most of the time the cars parked there do not have the Disabled Person sticker on the windshield and are not entitled to park there. Last week, a sprightly young man pulled ahead of me and parked in the last available Disabled Person space, and when I called out that the space was for disabled people, he yelled back, as he bounded up the steps into the hospital, "I am disabled...I can't read!"

Possible Solutions

Just inside the hospital there is a security guard at the front desk. Would it not be possible to have the guard regularly check this reserved parking area? If the guard is not licensed to issue parking tickets, perhaps the local police could be called. Another possible solution would be to post a "Violators Will Be Towed" sign and call a tow-truck to haul the car away. This is the policy at the mall, so I always find a space there.

I look forward to hearing from you and learning what solutions you are able to implement so that I, and other patients with similar challenges, can continue to access the resources of your hospital.

Sincerely,

Make Memos and Letters Scannable

The following memo requests some very detailed information. Unfortunately, written as it is, the reader may overlook some of the key requirements.

TO: Sylvia Harris

FROM: Gary Flanagan

RE: Annual Sales Meeting

Please contact Mr. John Murphy at the Fulton Plaza Hotel and get this information for me no later than next Tuesday morning. I will need to know the room and meal costs for 360 people and 180 double rooms for two nights and three days, costs per person per day, if there are any, for the recreational facilities at the hotel, and the fee for the Grand Banquet Hall for the three days. In addition, I will need you to arrange for some special equipment for the Banquet Hall for the three days, specifically a cordless microphone, an overhead projector and large screen, and a TV set and VCR.

Thank you for your prompt attention to this request.

Here is a "scannable" version of the same information:

TO: Sylvia Harris

FROM: Gary Flanagan

RE: Arrangements for Annual Sales Meeting July 16-18

Sylvia: please contact John Murphy at the Fulton Plaza Hotel and get this information for me by Tuesday:

- Room & meal costs for 360 people & 180 double rooms for two nights and three days
- Costs for recreational facilities at the hotel (if any)
- Costs for the Grand Banquet Hall for these three days

Also, I will need you to arrange for some special equipment for the Banquet Hall for the three days:

- A cordless microphone
- An overhead projector and large screen
- A TV set and VCR

Thanks, Sylvia, for all your help with these details!

MAKING IT SCANNABLE

Consider how you might reformat the following memo for the reader's eye, breaking the information down into headings and lists.

Memo 1

RE: Technical Manual Writing Procedure

There is a problem with the procedure in writing technical manuals as the current procedure is very confusing and time-consuming. At present, writers gather data from technical leads and write a first draft, which is then returned to the technical leads, who make changes and additions. From this point on, there is no direct line of development. Sometimes the draft is sent to the graphics department to insert the necessary illustrations, then returned to the writers, who make changes, and then on to the final editor, who again makes changes that require the graphics to be changed…so the manual-in-progress circulates forever.

I have a suggestion for a new procedure: that the writers interview technical leads for data; write the first draft; return draft to technical leads to review. Technical leads will then return the draft to writers who will make the necessary text changes. Writers would then pass the first draft on to the editor. The word processor would make the editing changes and produce a second draft, which would then be sent to graphics to illustrate and insert graphics. The final version would then be returned to the editor for final review and for sign-off to technical leads, quality assurance, and executive staff.

This procedure is used in several other companies that produce technical manuals, and is very effective. I am strongly in favor of implementing this procedure here, as our present (lack of) procedure is chaotic.

A scannable format

RE: Proposal for New Technical Manual Writing Procedure

Our current technical manual writing procedure is ineffective and confusing. I am therefore proposing this new procedure to improve—and shorten!—the process:

1. Writers interview technical leads.
2. Writers write first draft.
3. Technical leads review first draft.
4. Writers make necessary changes.
5. Editor edits first draft.
6. Word processor makes editing changes and produces second draft.
7. Graphic artist illustrates document and inserts graphics into second draft.
8. Editor reviews final draft and obtains sign-offs from:
   • Technical leads
   • Quality assurance
   • Executive staff

This procedure has proven effective in other organizations, and I am confident it will help here.

Another option, using a horizontal format

RE: Proposal for New Technical Manual Writing Procedure

Our current technical manual writing procedure is ineffective and confusing. I am therefore proposing this new procedure to improve—and shorten!—the process:

Responsibility	Action
Writers	1. Interview technical leads. 2. Write first draft.
Technical Leads	1. Review first draft.
Writers	1. Make necessary changes to first draft.
Editor	1. Edits first draft.
Word Processor	1. Enters changes to first draft. 2. Produces second draft.
Graphic Artist	1. Illustrates document and inserts graphics into second draft. 2. Produces final draft.
Editor	1. Reviews final draft. 2. Obtains sign-offs from: • Technical leads • Quality assurance • Executive staff

Note: This procedure has proven effective in other organizations, and I am confident it will help here.

MAKING IT SCANNABLE

Memo 2

Here is another example. See what techniques you can use to make this memo more "scannable."

TO: Marnie Graham

RE: Request for New Copy Machine

Please consider this memo as a follow-up to our brief conversation of this past week in which I mentioned that we need a new copy machine for our Southern Division in Springfield. At the present time, there is a small copy machine which we use on an almost continuous basis, but it is totally inadequate for our needs. Some of the staff often stay late just to copy material needed for the next day. We need a substantially larger machine, preferably one which is able to do enlarging, reducing, collating, and stapling, and has an automatic feeder and duplex feature.

In addition, please take note that, due to the fact that we reproduce not only reports, training outlines, and lesson plans for our many corporate-wide EAP training programs, but also create all of our own EAP forms as well, we have a heavy volume of usage.

I understand that this purchase would come out of Capital Budget, and as such, we must be placed on a waiting list. I would appreciate your attention to this request. If you have any further questions, please do not hesitate to call me.

A scannable format

TO: Marnie Graham

RE: Request for New Copy Machine

I spoke with you briefly last week and requested a new copy machine for our Southern Division in Springfield. Here are the specifics:

Big Problem!

Our present machine is small and inadequate for our needs. We need a substantially larger machine, preferably with these features:

- enlarging
- reducing
- stapling
- collating
- duplex feature
- automatic feeder

We Print a Lot!

We produce reports, outlines, manuals and lesson plans for our corporate-wide EAP training programs. In addition, we produce all our own EAP forms.

I understand that this purchase would come out of Capital Budget, and we will be placed on the waiting list. We badly need a new copier, Marnie, and we appreciate your help.

MAKING IT SCANNABLE

Memo 3

Here is another example. See what techniques you can use to make this memo "scannable."

Dear Shareholder:

It is an honor and a privilege to announce the distribution being released today of the Martin Investment Fund's Dividend Reinvestment Plan, a plan which will offer shareholders a number of advantages. Most importantly, this Plan will provide shareholders with the means of building holdings in the Fund and gaining the potential benefits of compounded investment returns. When a dividend or capital gains distribution is paid, it will be automatically reinvested in additional shares of the Fund and the compounding effect created through this reinvestment can substantially enhance returns.

Other benefits from participation in the Plan include convenience, due to the fact that Fund shares will be automatically purchased for participants. In addition, participants will be able to build holdings in the Fund at reduced or no brokerage costs. Participants will also find this automatic investment Plan more efficient and time-saving, and will receive, on a monthly basis, an account statement which will show total dividends, any capital gains distribution, date of investment, and number of shares purchased.

Should you be interested in participating in this Plan, kindly contact your brokerage firm or bank and request that they file an application on your behalf.

If you should have any questions or need additional information, please call the Martin Investment Fund at 1-800-555-4242.

Thank you for your continued support of the Fund.

A more scannable format

Dear Shareholder:

We have some exciting news for you!

You can now participate in the Martin Investment Fund's Dividend Reinvestment Plan, which will enable shareholders to automatically build holdings in the Fund and benefit from compounded investment returns.

How does this work?

When a dividend or capital gains distribution is paid, it will automatically be reinvested in additional shares of the Fund. This compounding effect can substantially increase your returns.

Participating in the Plan has other benefits!

> **More Convenient.** Fund shares will be automatically purchased for participants.

> **Less Expensive.** Participants will be able to build holdings in the Fund at reduced or no brokerage costs.

> **More Efficient.** Participants have no paperwork, and will receive a monthly account statement showing total dividends, any capital gains distribution, date of investment, and number of shares purchased.

Interested in participating in this Plan?

Please contact your brokerage firm or bank and ask them to file an application on your behalf.

If you have any questions, please contact me at the Martin Investment Fund a 1-800-555-4242.

As always, thank you for your continued support of the Fund.

Make Email Effective

Today, thanks to email, information moves with the speed of light. Because it is easy to use, many people dash off rambling messages that fall somewhere between a friendly chat and carefully chosen words using perfectly correct grammar. Email and the Internet have changed the way we read. Eighty percent of "netizens"—email and Internet users—scan for meaning. Here are some pointers to consider before you push "SEND":

Always

➤ Write a Subject Line with impact so your mail will be read.

➤ Be concise. Write short declarative sentences. Write the way you speak.

➤ Try to keep the message to just one screen (approximately 250 spaces).

➤ For longer messages, summarize on the first screen.

➤ Limit the message to just one subject.

Remember your "Netiquette"

➤ When communicating by email, all you see is a computer screen—no facial expressions, no voice on the phone. So always check your message for tone and possible misinterpretations.

➤ Email is a permanent record. Don't send anything with potential legal implications or risk copyright or licensing infringement.

➤ Always edit and proof for correctness. Respect your reader's time: missing caps and punctuation, misspellings and mistakes in grammar and word usage distract your reader. The written word represents you and your organization.

➤ If asking questions, itemize your inquiries with numbers or letters. This will make it easier for the recipient to provide itemized responses.

➤ Before sending an angry message, go have a cup of coffee and reconsider.

Email Shorthand

BCNU	be seeing you	OTOH	on the other hand
BTW	by the way	TIA	thanks in advance
f2f	face to face	ROTFL	rolling on the floor laughing
IOW	in other words	HHOK	Ha Ha!– only kidding!
FWIW	for what it's worth	TMOT	trust me on this
IMHO	in my humble opinion	TTYTT	to tell you the truth
CUL	see you later	WADR	with all due respect
TPTB	the powers that be	LOL	laughing out loud
FTR	for the record		TYPING IN ALL CAPS = SHOUTING!

A NOTE ON WEBSITES

Only 16% of netizens actually read Web pages word-for-word. Most scan for meaning. Therefore, design and write your website content to deliver maximum impact with minimum words.

When designing a website

➤ Write scannable text: terse, tight.

➤ State the purpose in the first line.

➤ Use headings and labels.

➤ Highlight key words.

A P P E N D I X

Punctuation Update

Punctuate for your reader's eye. Use punctuation creatively to subordinate less important information so your reader can skim.

1. **Parentheses and colons** can be used to visually break up strings of difficult-to-read commas and semicolons. Consider the difference punctuation makes in the following examples.

   Awkward: The regional sales managers who attended the conference were Alice Martin, North; Bob Gomez, South; Bruce Graham, East; and Ivy Chiu, West.

   Easier: Several regional sales managers attended the conference: Alice Martin (North); Bob Gomez (South); Bruce Graham (East); and Ivy Chiu (West).

   Awkward: Three sections of the report were of interest to me, particularly the discussion of next quarter's projected sales at the beginning of Section II, the outline of the new advertising campaign in Europe in Section III, and the plans for enlarging our laboratory facilities in Canada at the end of Section IV.

   Easier: I found three sections of the report of special interest: the discussion of next quarter's projected sales (p.2); the outline of the new European advertising campaign (p.6); and the plans for enlarging our lab facilities in Canada (p.8).

2. **Use dashes** to make important or dramatic information stand out.

   Ho-Hum: Jane Metcalfe is taking an extended leave because she is going to run for mayor.

   Impactful: Jane Metcalfe is taking an extended leave of absence–she's going to run for mayor!

   Ho-Hum: I am of the opinion that this merger is the correct move at this point in time.

   Impactful: I think–no, I am positive!–this merger is the right move at the right time.

Punctuation Update (CONTINUED)

3. **Avoid run-on sentences;** they confuse readers. The most common punctuation mistake in business writing is run-on sentences with therefore, meanwhile, nevertheless, however, and other conjunctive adverbs.

   When a run-on sentence is caused by putting two separate thoughts together, you can simplify it by correct use of punctuation—either using a semicolon or inserting a period to create two sentences. In the following examples, the two separate thoughts are underlined.

   <u>We no longer have that item in stock</u>, therefore <u>we are returning your check.</u>

   This can be solved in two ways—either by making two sentences (A) or by using a semicolon (B):

   A. We no longer have that item in stock. Therefore, we are returning your check.

   B. We no longer have that item in stock; therefore, we are returning your check.

   <u>Ms. Wilson will attend the meeting</u>, however, <u>she will not attend the dinner.</u>

   A. Ms. Wilson will attend the meeting. However, she will not attend the dinner.

   B. Ms. Wilson will attend the meeting; however, she will not attend the dinner.

4. **Don't distract your reader with apostrophe catastrophes.** Make sure you are using them correctly. Some real-life examples:

Incorrect	Correct
Store sign: Best Bagel's on Broadway!	Bagels
Cover letter: Our Newsletter was created for companies like your's!	yours
Company sign: Employee's Cafeteria	Employees'
Sales letter: Our new software is popular because of it's ease of use	its

5. **Hyphenate for your reader's eye.** When compound adjectives come before the noun, it's easier to read if they are hyphenated.

Confusing	Better
I flew first class.	I had a first-class ticket.
The project had a big budget.	It was a big-budget project.
I work part time.	I have a part-time job.
John's writing is well known.	John is a well-known writer.

Punctuation Update (CONTINUED)

6. Hyphenate items in a series.

"There are both full- and part-time positions available."

"We need 5-, 10-, and 20-gallon drums."

"The performance was attended by 5-, 6-, and 7-year-old students."

7. Use a comma after a long introductory phrase or to separate an otherwise confusing introduction. Notice the confusion caused by missing commas.

Confusing:	As we were barbecuing a snake crawled under the picnic table.
Better:	As we were barbecuing, a snake crawled under the picnic table.
Confusing:	I had an argument with my boss. The day after I quit my job.
Better:	I had an argument with my boss. The day after, I quit my job.
Confusing:	After being delivered to the side entrance to the construction site the tools were unpacked.
Better:	After being delivered to the side entrance to the construction site, the tools were unpacked.

Proofreading Tips

1. It is easy to miss errors on a computer screen. For important documents, proof from hard copy.

2. Print out in double space. It will be easier to read and you will have room to mark changes on your printout.

3. Read it aloud, word by word. Some people even read it backward, word by word.

4. Let it get cold. Go have a cup of coffee, chat with a co-worker, or have lunch. Then come back with fresh eyes. You'll pick up errors you didn't see before.

5. Give it to another pair of eyes. Develop a Proofing Partnership with co-workers whose eyes you trust. They will see mistakes you may have missed.

6. Don't edit when you proof. Edit for grammar, syntax, clarity, and style first. Then go back and proof for spelling, punctuation, and capitalization.

7. Use your spellchecker, but don't rely on it 100%.

8. Proof at prime time. Never proof when you're tired.

9. Print out the final draft and check the visual design. Is the format reader-friendly?

Numbers in Writing

➤ Spell out numbers 1-10. Use figures for numbers above 10.

> *"The three reports were at least 25 pages each."*

➤ Use numbers for 1-10 when it will help comprehension or for technical significance.

> *"The score was 5 to 6."*
>
> *"A 30-year mortgage"*
>
> *"There is no charge for delivery in a 5-mile radius."*
>
> *"We received your order for a 6' x 8' carpet."*

➤ Use the same style in a related sequence.

> *"We have 3 factories, 11 regional offices, and 15 distribution centers."*
>
> *"From $750,000 to $1,000,000 (Not: $1 million)"*

➤ Use a combination of numbers and words when two figures are next to each other:

> *"12 forty-page reports"*
>
> *"six 10-gallon drums"*
>
> *"525 Fifth Avenue"*

➤ Use a combination of numbers and words to express high amounts.

> *"The population of India is 980 million (easier than 980,000,000)."*

➤ In formal correspondence, spell out numbers of 1 or 2 words.

    "I interviewed twenty-three applicants for the position."

    "Over three hundred people attended the conference."

➤ Exception to above: when numbers would require more than two words.

    "There were 357 people at the conference."

➤ Spell out a number that begins a sentence.

    "Seven hundred people signed the petition."

➤ Exception to above: when the number is normally used in numerical form only.

    "1999 was our best sales year."

➤ Omit the decimal point and zeros in a sentence.

    "I enclose my check for $145 for the order."

➤ Include the zeros in a column of figures.

    $168.15
    225.00
     42.38

Page 98

TEST YOUR WORD USAGE

Mistakes in word usage distract readers from your intended message. Test your skill by circling the correct word usage for each of these sentences.

1. Joan never (wavers/waivers) when making a decision.

2. He bought her a 10-(carrot/karat/caret/carat) diamond.

3. The argument is between Vicki and (he/him).

4. His tie (complements/compliments) his suit and shirt nicely.

5. The (capitol/capital) of Florida is Tallahassee.

6. Neither Jack nor I (are/am) going to the conference.

7. The company is divided into three (discrete/discreet) branches.

8. I asked (everyone/every one) in my office to the party, and (everyone/every one) of them came.

9. (Who/Whom) shall I say is calling?

10. He called to find out if I (were/was) available for a meeting.

11. Each of the reports (contain/contains) several errors.

12. The policy will take (effect/affect) next week but will (effect/affect) only part-time employees.

13. His speech (invoked/evoked) cheers from the audience.

14. A magazine published twice a month is a (semi-monthly/bi-monthly).

15. The report is not ready today(,/;) however (,/;) we'll send it out tomorrow.

16. In his speech, John (inferred/implied) he would run for office.

17. If I (would have known/had known) his number, I would have called him.

18. My neighbor (continually/continuously) borrows things from me.

19. He was (appraised/apprised) of the accident this morning.

20. I need to speak to (whoever/whomever) is in charge of the project.

Compare your answers to those on page 102.

Author's Suggested Responses to Exercises

Talk to Your Reader (Page 26-27)

1. Enclosed is our new product brochure!

2. Here's my check for $125 for…

3. Please send the outstanding balance by June 15.

4. If you need more information, please call me.

The author's suggestion for a more conversational letter:

> Enclosed is your endorsement effective April 1, 2000 amending your home insurance policy #541023. Please take a few minutes to review it, noting the terms, conditions, and exclusions, and then attach it to your policy. If you find any discrepancies or have questions, please call me.
>
> It's always a pleasure to serve your insurance needs.

Practice Being Positive (Page 31)

1. We deliver up to 11pm.

2. Please observe the safety codes.

3. If payment is received before May 1, there will be no penalty.

4. We'll ship your order as soon as we receive your payment.

5. Please be sure to send…

6. Your available credit is $5,000.

The author's suggestions for a more positive tone:

> Enclosed is a Policyholder's Report form which was previously sent to you but perhaps was mislaid. Please complete this form and return it to us promptly so that your premium can be adjusted to reflect actual exposures.
>
> Please call us if you need help completing the form.

Time to De-Jargonize (Page 37)

1. The supervisor will meet with the union representatives on Thursday.

2. We'll help out whenever possible.

3. The company bus connects our Miami and Ft. Lauderdale offices.

4. Employees who come in late will be subject to our lateness policy.

5. For best gas mileage, drive under 55mph.

6. She said "no."

Constructing Parallel Sentences (Page 41)

1. Forms should be read first, accurately completed, and returned to us.

2. Joan was concerned about salary, security, and job advancement.

3. Bob enjoys skiing, hiking, and camping in the mountains on the weekends.

4. I found it easier to write the report than to edit it.

5. This year's sales were better than last year's.

6. John handled the crisis quickly, thoroughly and professionally.

7. His lack of enthusiasm is disappointing, frustrating, and annoying.

Practice the Active Approach (Page 49)

1. We'll ship your order as soon as we receive your payment.

2. All employees will attend the meeting.

3. The engineer repaired the conveyor belt.

4. The shipping department has confirmed the delivery dates..

5. Bruce Graham compiled the research, and Mark Ayton wrote the report.

The author's suggestion for a more active voice:

All new employees must send copies of their health records to Kate Smith in Central Records by January 5. Please include records of immunization and vaccinations.

Do observe the January 5 deadline, as we cannot guarantee health coverage if we don't have your records.

If you need more information, call John Jones at X123.

Create Must-Read Reference Lines (Page 61-62)

Re: Big Problems in the Warehouse!

Re: You're Invited!

Re: Meeting Time Change!

Write Shorter Paragraphs (Page 67)

John: I recently found out that the LA Division has an increasingly serious problem with employee turnover. Many highly skilled employees are leaving for companies that offer:

- Flex-time hours to avoid severe rush-hour traffic on the freeways

- Telecommuting from home 1-2 days a week

- Day-care/after-school care for children

Can we meet Tuesday or Wednesday afternoon to discuss setting up some/all of these programs? Call me to set up a time. (71 words)

Test Your Word Usage (Page 98)

1. wavers
2. carat
3. him
4. complements
5. capital
6. am
7. discrete
8. everyone/every one
9. Who
10. was
11. contains
12. effect/affect
13. evoked
14. semi-monthly
15. ; however,
16. implied
17. had known
18. continually
19. apprised
20. whoever

Recommended Reading

Barzun, Jacques. *Simple & Direct: A Rhetoric for Writers*. New York: Harper, 1994.

Bozek, Phillip E. *50 One-Minute Tips to Better Communication*. Menlo Park, CA: Crisp Publications, 1997.

Brock, Susan L. *Better Business Writing*. Menlo Park, CA: Crisp Publications, 1997.

Brill, Laura. *Business Writing Quick and Easy*. New York: AMACOM. 1989.

Johnson, Edward D. *The Handbook of Good English*. New York: Washington Square Press, 1991.

Joseph, Albert. *Put It in Writing: Learn How to Writer Clearly, Quickly, and Persuasively*. New York: McGraw-Hill, 1998.

Lauchman, R. *Plain Style: Techniques for Simple, Concise, Emphatic Business Writing*. New York: AMACOM, 1993.

Lederer, Richard, and Richard Dowis. *The Write Way: Choice Words, Phrases, Sentences, and Paragraphs for Every Situation*. New York: Pocket Books, 1995.

Maggio, Rosalie. *How to Say It*. Upper Saddle River, NJ: Prentice Hall, 1990.

Sabin, William A. *The Gregg Reference* Manual. New York: McGraw-Hill, 2000.

Tarshis, Barry. *Grammar for Smart People: Your User-Friendly Guide to Speaking and Writing Better English*. New York: Pocket Books, 1993.

Zinsser, William. *On Writing Well: The Classic Guide to Writing Nonfiction*. New York: Harper, 1998.

Now Available From

Books•Videos•CD-ROMs•Computer-Based Training Products

Subject Areas Include:

Management
Human Resources
Communication Skills
Personal Development
Marketing/Sales
Organizational Development
Customer Service/Quality
Computer Skills
Small Business and Entrepreneurship
Adult Literacy and Learning
Life Planning and Retirement